DEDICATION AND ACKNOWLEDGMENTS

Dedication—To my mother, for buying me my first tarantula and encouraging my unique interests ever since.

Acknowledgments—I would like to thank the staff of the Bergenfield Pet Shop for their cooperation, Alice Gray of the American Museum of Natural History, my sister Claire for her help in typing the manuscript, my brother Peter for his services as a photographer, and especially my whole family for their patience and support which made this book a reality.

Cover photos by
Dr. Herbert R. Axelrod
© 1981 by T.F.H. Publications, Inc., Ltd.

Distributed in the UNITED STATES by T.F.H. Publications, Inc., 211 West Sylvania Avenue, Neptune City, NJ 07753; in CANADA by H & L Pet Supplies Inc., 27 Kingston Crescent, Kitchener, Ontario N2B 2T6; Rolf C. Hagen Ltd., 3225 Sartelon Street, Montreal 382 Quebec; in ENGLAND by T.F.H. (Great Britain) Ltd., 11 Ormside Way, Holmethorpe Industrial Estate, Redhill, Surrey RH1 2PX; in AUSTRALIA AND THE SOUTH PACIFIC by Pet Imports Pty. Ltd., Box 149, Brookvale 2100 N.S.W., Australia; in NEW ZEALAND by Ross Haines & Son, Ltd., 18 Monmouth Street, Grey Lynn, Auckland 2 New Zealand; in SINGAPORE AND MALAYSIA by MPH Distributors Pte., 71-77 Stamford Road, Singapore 0617; in the PHILIPPINES by Bio-Research, 5 Lippay Street, San Lorenzo Village, Makati, Rizal; in SOUTH AFRICA by Multipet Pty. Ltd., 30 Turners Avenue, Durban 4001. Published by T.F.H. Publications Inc., Ltd., the British Crown Colony of Hong Kong. THIS IS THE 1983 EDITION.

TARANTULAS

JOHN G. BROWNING

Tarantula spinning silk. Photo by Ron Reagan.

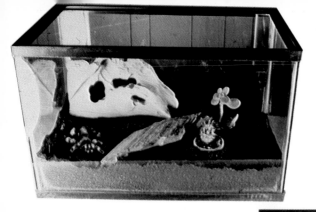

Above: A typical tarantularium made from an aquarium.
Right: Don't be fooled; tarantulas can bite, so learn how to handle them *before* picking them up. Photos by Dr. Herbert R. Axelrod.

Introduction

TARANTULA MANIA

If you enjoy keeping pet tarantulas, you share your esoteric taste in pets with many others. From scientists to students to secretaries, ordinary people all around the country (and even the world) are going to pet stores and buying tarantulas. Curiosity is rapidly replacing fear when dealing with these creatures; people who used to shiver at the sight of tarantulas now gladly pluck dollar bills from their pockets in exchange for one of these large spiders. Why?

If there's one thing that is sure to stir the wheels of human fascination, it is a novelty. Although it doesn't yet have enough adherents to be called a fad, the keeping of tarantulas as pets is certainly growing in popularity, and the market for tarantulas is rapidly growing. Tom Krause, a pet store proprietor from Elk Grove Village, Illinois, said in September, 1976 that since the beginning of 1976 his pet shop had sold 800 tarantulas. This reportedly shows a 25% increase since 1975. A *World Book Encyclopedia* article quotes him as saying, "Very few people walk into the shop to buy tarantulas, but when they see them they are intrigued."

According to an article in the July 17, 1979 *National Enquirer*, tarantulas have become even more popular in recent years. Mrs. Vonda Mosley of the wholesaling firm of Gators of Miami was quoted as saying, "Demand for tarantulas is booming. We get about 500 tarantulas every six or eight weeks, and they sell very quickly. I expect our sales will be 500 or more a month quite soon." The firm of Wilson Pet Supply in Bensenville, Ill., sold between 4000 and 5000 tarantulas in the latter half of 1978, as well as thousands so far this year. In the same article, David Van Bodegraven, of Pet Ranch Imports in Tucson, Arizona, revealed that his company sold 10,000 tarantulas in 1978.

To cope with the demand for tarantulas, a multitude of new companies have sprung up. According to several sources, tarantulas sell especially well during the Christmas and (suprisingly) Valentine's Day holidays. The sole non-profit organization in this sea of lucrative business ventures is the American Tarantula Society, which is described further on in the book.

Selling tarantulas themselves is not the only way to profit from these spiders. Tarantula venom is sometimes used by pharmaceutical companies in the production of antivenins. An acquaintance of mine from a Florida serpentarium regularly performs the duty of "milking" venom out of snakes and also from tarantulas (occasionally). Tarantula T-shirts, iron-on transfers, buttons and greeting cards are selling well throughout the country. There have been four tarantula books, in addition to my own; one is out of print, two are intended for young children, and the other (Dale Lund's *All About Tarantulas)* would make a welcome addition to any tarantula enthusiast's library.

Tarantula profits are not earned solely by merchandise; money has been made providing various services. In California, a San Francisco jewelry store that fell prey to repeated break-ins contacted a security agency. This firm rented tarantulas to the jewelry store and posted signs warning people of the poisonous sentries, and the jeweler's problems ceased. I myself operate TARANTULA ENTERPRISES, a firm which will rent tarantulas to jewelry stores and department stores, as well as private individuals. We will also promote and publicize establishments which sell tarantulas as pets and are available for live demonstrations, features and educational lectures.

Yet another sign of growing interest in tarantulas is the recent influx of TV movies and weekly episodes featuring tarantula themes. Unfortunately, the majority of these themes serve only to exploit the tarantula's bad reputation, not to educate the viewer on the better side of these unusual pets.

MY TARANTULAS

At the moment, I possess six tarantulas: two male Mexican red-legs (Genghis and Himmler), one female Honduras black velvet (Attila), one male Haitian (Tamerlane), a male Texas cinnamon (Idi Amin), and one immature red-toe bird-eating spider (Mengele). These tarantulas, collected over a period of two years, are a source of great joy and pride to me. I look upon them as not just pets but also as conversation pieces, business associates and hairy but fascinating little friends from whom a great deal can be learned. It is sometimes very difficult for me to discuss my tarantulas without sounding coldly clinical or ruthlessly businesslike or like a pet owner who pampers his animals.

As I sat down to begin this book, I took the time to recall arachnid-related experiences that stand out in my memory: the day my mother (after a great deal of coaxing, convincing, and persuading) bought me my first tarantula, Genghis; the occasions on which my tarantulas won ribbons in open pet competition; the formation of my firm, Tarantula Enterprises; the escape and recapture of my venomous bark scorpion, Vlad; and the day I became a member of the American Tarantula Society.

Tarantulas make excellent pets and need only one feeding per week to stay plump and healthy. The tarantula on the facing page is in great shape, while the tarantula above is getting old. Photos by Ron Reagan.

At this point, many people have probably formed a question in their minds: why a tarantula? Well, a tarantula requires very little care. It needs perhaps one feeding per week, in addition to keeping fresh water always on hand. There is no messy problem of walking it; a tarantula excretes a quick-drying, odorless material. It carries no diseases communicable to people or domestic livestock, and for that reason it can be transported internationally. It is a noiseless creature and is actually quite docile. Its bite is relatively harmless to humans, and it avoids contact with people as much as possible. In short, it is a unique, fascinating pet.

The purpose of this book is not only to show how misunderstood the tarantula is but also to illustrate the fact that it makes a wonderful pet. This book is intended to aid the reader who already has a tarantula, but hopefully it will also help the reader who is thinking of buying a tarantula.

Spiders, like those shown
above and to the right, belong
to the class Arachnida and
are related to scorpions and
ticks. Many are annoying
animals, and many are
venomous. Handle all of them
carefully.

Tarantulas In General

Tarantulas are spiders. Like all other spiders, they are arachnids, that is, they are grouped by taxonomists in the class Arachnida—scorpions, mites, ticks and daddy longlegs as well as some less well known animals.

There are hundreds of species of tarantulas throughout the world. They can be found in the arid desert regions of Mexico and the southwestern United States, the lush tropical rain forests of South and Central America and the exotic Caribbean islands. Various species of tarantulas inhabit areas of Africa and the Indian subcontinent as well as northern Australia. In the United

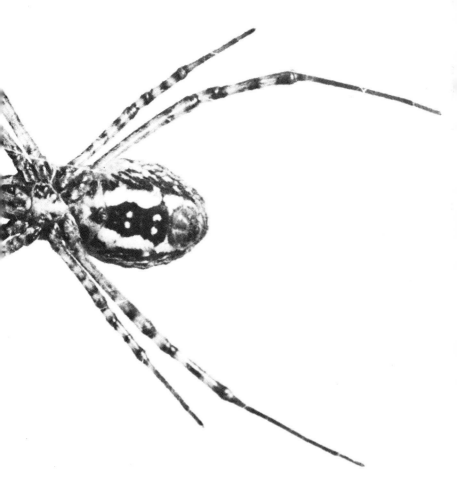

CEPHALOTHORAX

PEDIPALP

CHELICERA

EYES

CARAPACE

APODEME **ANUS**

SPINNERETS

ABDOMEN

External anatomy of a tarantula as viewed from above.

14

CEPHALOTHORAX

PEDIPALP

CHELICERA

States there are about 30 species of tarantulas. They primarily inhabit Arizona, New Mexico, Texas and Nevada. However, tarantulas have been found in southern California, Utah, Arkansas and even parts of Kansas. In fact, tarantulas range all the way up the Mississippi River, but as a rule they are never seen east of this waterway (except as pets, of course).

In the wild, tarantulas dwell in a variety of locations. Burrowing tarantulas construct silk-lined tunnels of varying length. One California burrowing species makes a small tower out of earth, grass and twigs at the opening to its abode. It uses this "observation point" to spot potential insect prey. Tree-dwelling tarantulas build elaborate aerial nests out of silk. Tarantulas have been found near human dwellings, on hillsides and in rockpiles.

TARANTULA ANATOMY

Having a working knowledge of your tarantula's anatomy will not only aid in keeping it healthy but will also prove helpful when concocting answers to the questions of interested friends and family. There will probably be a great deal of interest generated by your unusual pet, so this section is intended to help you satisfy that curiosity.

The body is composed of two major parts, the *abdomen* and the *cephalothorax*. These two sections are joined together by a "pedicel," or waist. Both main sections have parts attached to them. The abdomen has two pairs of spinnerets, and the cephalothoracic appendages include four pairs of walking legs.

The Cephalothorax

The cephalothorax itself is the junction at which all eight legs are joined. The cephalothorax houses the central nervous system, brain and sucking stomach, which plays a vital role in the tarantula's digestive system. The cephalothorax contains the carapace, the chelicerae and fangs, mouth, eyes, apodeme and pedipalpi.

CARAPACE: The carapace is situated on top of the cephalothorax and shields it. Located on the carapace are the tarantula's eight eyes. Depending on the species, a tarantula's carapace can range in color from a stunning purple to a striking greenish black.

MOUTH: The tarantula's mouth is located on its underside, and its reddish-brown color is readily distinguishable.

APODEME: The apodeme is a small, crater-like depression located in the middle of the carapace. It is at this point that the leg muscles are connected.

CHELICERAE and FANGS: The chelicerae are two thick appendages extending from the head. They are used in hunting down and killing prey. A fang is situated at the end of each chelicera . On most of my tarantulas, the fangs are about half an inch long. The fangs of a tarantula point straight down, unlike the fangs of other spiders, which criss-cross. When killing prey, a paralyzing venom from the poison glands (located in the chelicerae) races through the chelicerae to the hollow fangs, where it is injected into the hapless victim. The same fluid helps break down the tissue of the prey in order to aid in the digestive process.

PEDIPALPI: The pedipalpi resemble miniature legs and are located in the front of the tarantula. Their most important function is served during the mating season. Palpal bulbs situated on the end of each pedipalp store the male tarantula's sperm prior to mating. The pedipalpi are also used as sense organs, since they probe ahead and perceive potential prey. I have even noticed my tarantulas using these appendages to "shovel" crickets towards their fangs when feeding. One spider in particular, Attila, even uses her pedipalpi to pin down one cricket while devouring another. The pedipalpi are used to help clean the tarantula's fangs.

LEGS: The tarantula's eight legs enable it to maneuver quickly around numerous obstacles. The two claws at the tip of each segmented leg enable the tarantula to climb over rocks and onto walls. On many occasions, I have observed my tarantulas scurrying up the glass or plastic walls of their homes. I've even seen them clinging upside down on the top of their tanks. Mengele, my South American tree-dwelling tarantula, is particularly agile; he walks and even hunts while clinging to the wall of his tank, occasionally leaving this aerial safety for a rare visit to the floor of the container. Since a tarantula's blood pressure is responsible for extending its legs, it is crucial that this pressure

Beauty lies in the eyes of the beholder, and tarantulas are beautiful—if you like spiders. Photos by Dr. Herbert R. Axelrod.

be constantly maintained. A lack of fluids in the spider's body can bring about a drastic drop in the pressure of the blood. Such a reduction would result in the tarantula's inability to walk.

The Abdomen

The other major section of the tarantula's body, the abdomen, contains a number of vital body systems. These include parts of the digestive system (digestive tube) and the circulatory system (heart) as well as the respiratory system (lungs and lung slits), the reproductive system (genital openings and ovaries) and the excretory system (spinnerets).

LUNGS: A tarantula possesses two pairs of lungs, as opposed to most spiders, which have only one pair. After air enters the lung slits, it passes through the four "book" lungs, so named because the slender folds of flesh resemble the pages of a book.

SPINNERETS: The spinnerets are small, finger-like appendages attached to the back of the abdomen. The tip of each spinneret consists of many tiny tubes. Through these tubes flow the liquid silk that is manufactured by the silk glands, contained in the abdomen. Upon being discharged from the silk tubes, the liquid silk is manipulated and spun into a thread by the spinnerets.

Senses

Because it is a hunter, the tarantula relies a great deal upon its sensory receptors. The most highly developed of these sensory apparatuses are undoubtedly the tarantula's hairs. These sensitive hairs aid in locating prey and are vital elements of the tarantula's nervous system. As for sight, a tarantula's eyes, however numerous, are extremely poor. Whether tarantulas can hear or not is debatable, but I have heard of one species in Texas that has been known to make barking noises. Tarantulas also have a sense of taste, and some pets will ignore offerings of mealworms or particularly offensive beetles. Do tarantulas also have a sense of smell? Look on the underside of your pet's leg joints and you will see the hairless white lyre organs. Some experts believe these to be the tarantula's organs of smell. It is a fact that during the mating season a female's scent can be detected by wandering males for miles around.

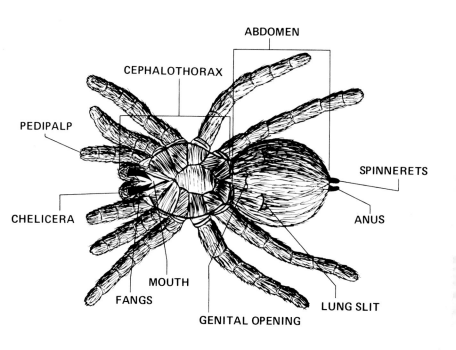

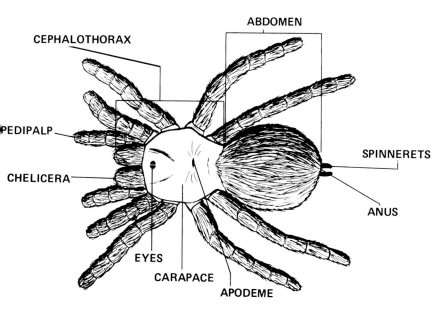

21

On the facing page, an African hunting wasp has paralyzed a baboon spider and is dragging it into its nest, where it will lay an egg on the paralyzed spider. As the egg hatches, the baby wasp will feed on the living but paralyzed spider. The photo above shows a more common wasp whose venom is histamine.

Identification

Unfortunately, the identification of different tarantula species is in a sorry state. Few people are willing to take the time and energy needed to conduct a proper study. Tarantulas must often be killed first in order for a correct taxonomic identification to be made. These two factors have hindered the expansion of knowledge concerning tarantulas and have resulted in considerable confusion among tarantula owners. For example, Mexican red-legs have been identified as both *Dugesiella hentzi* and *Aphonopelma emilia*. It gets to the point where even the experienced tarantula keeper is unsure of what he's keeping.

Regardless of what tarantulas are taxonomically, we should be aware that there are certain misconceptions regarding tarantulas in the mind of the public. I have had quite a job convincing people that tarantulas are not the deadly killers portrayed in movies. However repulsive they may appear to other people, I will always regard tarantulas as unique, intriguing accomplishments of nature.

TARANTULAS' NATURAL ENEMIES

Most tarantula owners need not be concerned with protecting their pets from the spiders' natural enemies. However, a number of tarantula enthusiasts live in areas where both the tarantula and its most dangerous natural enemy, the hunting wasp, exist. Moreover, the unique mode of combat that takes place between tarantulas and hunting wasps is certain to pique the interest of tarantula owners everywhere.

Hunting wasps differ from most other wasps in that they are not social insects; that is, each one is independent instead of being part of a wasp community. Among themselves, hunting wasps fall into a number of categories: bee-hunting wasps, caterpillar-hunting wasps, froghopper-hunting wasps, and spider-hunting wasps. In addition, the wasps are also classified according to the types of nests they build.

The spider-hunting wasps, of the family Pompilidae, are found in both tropical and temperate zones, from the cool green heaths of England to the sun-drenched North American deserts. The most familiar type belongs to the genus *Pepsis*.

Since the tropical wasps are among the largest wasps in the world, it is only fitting that they should prey upon tarantulas, which are among the world's largest spiders. Still, one needs only a quick look at these unusual gladiators to become convinced that it is a ridiculous mismatch. The wasp is scarcely 1/10 the size of an average tarantula; its only weapon is its stinger. The tarantula, on the other hand, is armed with superior size, a pair of poisonous fangs and eight legs.

The usual scenario for such a confrontation goes something like this: A female wasp, flying overhead in search of food for her offspring, spies a mild-mannered tarantula. The wasp immediately dives to the attack. Sensing impending danger through instinct, the tarantula rears up on its back legs in an attack position and bares its fangs. Undaunted, the wasp advances, and what follows resembles a boxing match in many respects. The two opponents circle about, venturing tentative strikes. The sharp fangs of the tarantula miss their mark for the last time, and at last the speedy hunting wasp sees its opening. It deftly sinks the stinger into the exposed nerve-centers on the undersurface of the unfortunate tarantula. Seized by the paralyzing effect of the wasp's venom, the tarantula slips into unconsciousness, a sleep from which it will never awaken.

The female wasp then drags the tarantula along the ground to a suitable location for a burrow. Once the burrow has been constructed, the helpless tarantula is pushed in. An egg from which a wasp larva will eventually emerge is laid on top of the spider. When the egg hatches, the larva begins feeding on this supply of living food. Due to the paralysis-inducing sting of the wasp, the hapless tarantula is literally eaten alive.

As grisly as it may appear, this is nature. However, the outcome is not always bad. In rare cases, the tarantula has emerged victorious in this life-and-death struggle. In slightly more common instances, a defeated and paralyzed tarantula may be too much for the average *Pepsis* wasp to transport. The spider is sometimes abandoned for game that is easier to bring home. Usually, however, the tarantula falls prey to wandering ants and beetles before it can "sleep off" the stun of the wasp venom. In one incident that just might be the only one of its kind, a wasp drag-

The author's two pet tarantulas, Genghis and Attila, are kept in individual plastic aquaria. Photo by Ron Reagan. On the facing page, a tarantula was placed on a piece of glass when it began to excrete its waste. This dried up quickly without odor. Photo by Dr. Herbert R. Axelrod.

ging a tarantula walked right into a jar held in the outstretched hand of a tarantula enthusiast! The dreaded wasp was killed and preserved; the tarantula recovered from the wasp injury after a few months "and lived happily ever after." Talk about the tables being turned!

THE MOLTING PROCESS

Molting (or moulting, as it is often spelled) is one of the most intriguing life functions of the tarantula. It is fascinating to watch the tarantula gradually work its way out of an old skin and emerge in a shiny new covering. My own tarantulas have molted a total of five times: twice for Attila, once each for Genghis, Tamerlane and Idi Amin. (Two of my tarantulas have not yet molted). Most species of tarantulas molt two to four times a year until they reach maturity. Upon reaching maturity, the average tarantula will molt once or twice a year.

The process of molting serves a multitude of purposes. It renews the tarantula's outer covering and even replaces "missing parts." That is, if your tarantula is missing any of its appendages, they will reappear during a molt. Keeping track of your tarantula's molts is important when you're attempting to breed tarantulas. A male tarantula acquires his mating "hooks" after one of his last molts. The female tarantula will often discourage a potential mate if she is due to molt soon. She is usually sluggish and "not in the mood" prior to a molt.

Many tarantula owners, including myself, have noticed certain behavioral and physical changes both before and after a molt. Tarantulas will refuse food for a week or two before molting but are often ravenous following the ordeal. About a week preceding the molt, the tarantula might drink a great deal of water, perhaps in anticipation of the dehydration that often sets in after the molting process is completed. Some tarantula owners have noticed droplets of a clear fluid "leaking" from leg joints before every molt. Probably the last signal that you will observe is a darkening of the abdomen, one of the signs of an impending molt.

At the very beginning of a molt, all movements on the part of the tarantula will cease. Bodily energy reserves which have been saved for just this moment are now used, as the tarantula slowly begins to withdraw itself from its own skin. The whole process takes less than 24 hours and leaves the tarantula with a shiny, moist new skin in place of an old, faded one. The tarantula is extremely sensitive after molting and should not be handled. It is best to offer food and fresh water at this time, but don't be surprised if your pet merely stretches out and rests. You may notice some bleeding after the molt. This bleeding must be tended to immediately in order to prevent death from loss of blood. Such bleeding is rare but it can happen.

The following is an eyewitness account of the molting of Attila, my Honduran black velvet. The observations recorded won't be the same as observations recorded for other species and will probably differ even from observations made of other Honduras black velvets. It is also interesting to note that Attila never gives a warning sign prior to a molt; I have seen her eating less than 24 hours before molting. She does not spin a silk bed just for molting; she uses the same resting area all year round. Because she is a black velvet tarantula, it is difficult to see a darkening of her abdomen.

August 15

3:30 p.m.—I first notice that Attila is on her back. Attila is the only one of my tarantulas to molt while on her back. All the other spiders molt while huddled against a corner of their tank on their side. Upon discovering the situation, I carefully placed her tank in a slightly warmer location.

4:00 p.m.—I notice that her legs are curled tightly inwards, toward her body. Upon touching her gently, I find that Attila's third left leg will move slightly. Her chelicerae and fangs are rigidly shut.

4:15 p.m.—No change in situation.

4:35 p.m.—There is a slight movement of fangs.

4:50 p.m.—The fangs gnash back and forth a second time.

5:00 p.m.—No movement.

5:15 p.m.—Again, no movement. This lack of movement continued until approximately 7:45 p.m., when movement beneath her body was noticed. Attila was continually active until about 8:50 p.m. By this time, she had withdrawn three legs. She

Prior to molting this tarantula (see facing page) began spinning a silken bed all over its aquarium home. The photo above shows a closeup of a tarantula guarding its egg sac. Photo by Ron Reagan.

On the facing page is a closeup of a tarantula spinning its bed, while above, a tarantula protects an egg sac. Photos by Ron Reagan.

abruptly stopped moving and remained motionless for seven minutes.

8:57 p.m.—Attila begins withdrawing again and does not stop until 9:30 p.m. At this time, she is on her side and all legs have been pulled out. I can see the fangs, which are white; her chelicerae, which are gnashing back and forth in a "chewing" motion; and the area around the chelicerae, which appears very red and raw.

9:40 p.m.—Attila is now moving in a slight rocking motion. She has discarded nearly all of her skin.

10:25 p.m.—Although Attila is totally disengaged, she remains very close to her old skin. The old skin is slightly larger than the living tarantula.

Two days passed before Attila's fangs darkened, and she then devoured all food offered.

REMEMBER: Molting is both a traumatic experience and an exhausting ordeal for any tarantulas. All movement ceases, and many life functions and senses are suspended during this period. DO NOT handle the tarantula during the molt or for several days afterwards.

Try to buy your tarantula from a pet store so you can get firsthand information and have the opportunity (see left) of learning how to handle it. Mail-order firms have their limitations and might very well send you (see below) a wild, poisonous unidentified spider that just looks like a tarantula.

Choosing Your Tarantula

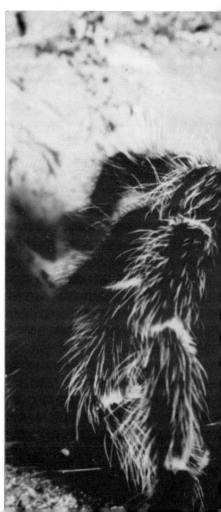

When you take that big step of buying your first tarantula (or adding another to your collection) you must be aware of certain factors that might influence your decision. First of all, where will you buy it? Although many pet stores stock at least a few tarantulas, quite a few do not. Normally those pet shops that don't stock tarantulas will order one for you, in which case your problem is solved. But if your local pet shop does not have tarantulas and won't order one for you, you can go to one of the mail-order exotic pet firms which carry an abundant and varied stock of tarantulas. When ordering tarantulas from a mail-order establishment, there are certain measures to take in order to get your money's worth:

Inquire as to whether the company guarantees live delivery. Many a tarantula owner has found himself stuck with a dead tarantula because time was not taken to read the "small print." You should have something in the form of a written guarantee that backs up the company's promises and sales talk. This will save money and work in the long run.

Inquire as to how long delivery will take. This will enable you to prepare for the tarantula's arrival and arrange living quarters and food. If delivery is late, you will also have exact dates to prove your claim.

Ask for the age and sex of the tarantula you're purchasing. Although the knowledge will probably come in handy, not all firms can be of help in this area.

Request any pamphlets, stock lists, catalogs, or any other available literature. These will also come in handy.

Check whether certain types of tarantulas offered are seasonal. This can cause a problem. Some spiders are available only during certain times of the year. To stay on the safe side, check first; it could save you valuable time and energy.

The issue of money is one of the most prominent when selecting a tarantula. Fifteen to twenty-five dollars is the usual cost for a tarantula, but price often varies from species to species and according to geographical location of the seller.

Long-lived or particularly colorful tarantulas usually command a higher price. This is true in the case of the Mexican red-leg. I have seen tarantulas, mostly old and sick-looking, priced as low as five dollars, and some range as high as $35.00-$40.00. I would advise paying no more than $25.00 dollars for a tarantula in good physical condition when buying your first specimen.

In order to get the most for your money, select a tarantula that will provide you with a maximum of enjoyment. Certain species have longer lifespans; one can live up to twenty years or more. On the other hand, many tarantulas rarely live past five or six years. In any case, I urge you to get either a female tarantula or an immature male one. This will greatly increase the chance of a longer lifespan. (For directions on telling the difference between the sexes, see the section on breeding.)

RECOMMENDED TARANTULA SPECIES

You have a variety of tarantula species to choose from. There are Mexican red-legs, Mexican red-abdomens, South American red-toes, Guatemalan red-backs, Mexican browns, Haitian blacks, Haitian curly-hairs, Honduran black velvets, Texas cinnamons, Guatemalan black velvets, and Haitian browns, to name but a few. The following is my own "top 5" list; it is based on my feelings and personal opinions. Admittedly, it reflects my own experience and differs in certain respects from the preferences of other tarantula enthusiasts.

The Mexican red-leg

This is by far the most commonly recommended—as pet or lab specimen—tarantula. It is one of the longer-lived tarantulas, with a lifespan of about 12 to 15 years. It is usually quite docile and can be handled easily. It is a very hardy creature and is also quite colorful. The red-leg is one of the larger tarantulas, having a five-inch to six-inch legspan. It is characterized by a black abdomen, black legs with bands of reddish orange and tan, and a black carapace that is bordered by tan coloration.

The Mexican brown

This also is a very docile tarantula. It is a dark brownish color and is slightly smaller than the red-leg. One of my favorite tarantulas, Heinrich, was a Mexican brown.

The Honduran black velvet

While it lacks the colorful patterns of the Mexican red-leg, the Honduran black velvet's striking jet-black appearance is almost as stunning. Although my own specimen is rather bad-tempered, many other tarantula enthusiasts have expressed great pleasure in handling these spiders. It has a relatively heavy build and roughly 4-inch to 6-inch legspan.

The Mexican blonde

This type of tarantula is one of the most gentle and easily handled spiders, despite its timidity. It has a pale beige appearance, with black bottom leg segments. It is a small tarantula, seldom exceeding four inches across the legs.

The South American red-toe

The South American red-toe is one of the so-called bird-eating spiders. This tree-dwelling tarantula has a slender build and small body. Its name is derived from the fact that the lower leg segment tips are colored with brilliant reddish pink and yellow hues. It is extremely agile but tends to be very nervous and jittery. Despite the latter, it makes an interesting addition to any tarantula buff's collection.

FOOD AND WATER NEEDS

Tarantulas kept in captivity have been known to have both voracious and finicky appetites. They have been seen devouring virtually every moving thing within their cage; yet at times they don't eat at all. Tarantulas have even been known to refuse certain kinds of live prey. In this manner, tarantulas are quite similar to the "higher" forms of animal life kept as pets.

In one way, tarantulas are very easy to feed: they will eat the same food for about as long as you keep them. Although it is nice to vary their diet once in a while, it is by no means necessary. Tarantulas will cheerfully devour nothing but large insects for their whole lifespan. While it is probably more convenient for you to stick with one staple food, a change in diet serves as both a learning experience for you and a refreshing change of pace for your tarantula.

Your pet requires live prey, although it will eat a dead insect or even ground chuck beef if it is jiggled to simulate movement and life. A tarantula will kill and eat large insects such as crickets, grasshoppers, beetles, roaches, etc. Being cannibalistic, a tarantula will eat another tarantula, as well as other kinds of spiders. Your tarantula can snatch large moths out of the air, hunt down frogs and lizards before your very eyes and pounce upon baby mice in a single bound! Not bad for a creature that sits motionless for days at a time! Tarantulas will also readily eat mealworms (beetle larvae). There is even one recorded instance of a tarantula with rather unusual feeding habits; this tarantula enjoyed eating fish! Because of a shortage of other living prey, small fish were placed in the tarantula's tank, and the tarantula gobbled them up enthusiastically. So you see, tarantulas will kill and eat a wide variety of prey.

I strongly recommend crickets as a source of nourishment for your tarantula. Many pet stores stock them as prey for small reptiles as well as tarantulas. They are usually priced cheaply enough even if bought singly, and they are often available at a special rate by the dozen or by the hundred. I would advise keeping a holding container exclusively for crickets, from which you can dole out a sufficient number for your tarantula. As you "fatten up" the crickets, you may even try your hand at raising them yourself. They will eat a wide variety of foods, but mine seem to especially like lettuce. Make sure that food is scattered throughout the cricket container and that a shallow dish of water is present. If you wish to breed crickets, keep a shallow container of moist sand in which the females can lay their eggs. After a successful mating, the female will deposit up to a hundred eggs, from which tiny baby crickets will emerge after several weeks. Be patient; it could be several months before the offspring are large enough for your tarantula to enjoy.

Most tarantulas require only one or two crickets a week. Many of the larger species will eat up to four or five each week. My Mexican red-legs sometimes devour as many as a half-dozen. When I acquired my first tarantula, Genghis, I put a dozen crickets in his cage. By the end of the day, all were dead and most were eaten. Don't worry about overfeeding your tarantula; it will eat according to its own needs of the moment. As for underfeeding, if the tarantula's abdomen is shriveled-looking, you should give it food and water. Tarantulas can survive for months without eating, and species which hibernate in the winter usually do. In experiments conducted by Dr. William J. Baerg, two tarantulas lived without food for 23 months and 27 months respectively.

The manner in which the tarantula stalks its prey is truly fascinating. I never tire of watching my tarantulas as they hunt and feed. Sometimes the spider will allow the cricket to actually walk under it, tempting fate. At other times, it will greedily attack the cricket as soon as it enters the tank. However, the tarantula usually waits until the cricket maneuvers into just the right position of vulnerability, and then . . . POUNCE! It seizes the cricket with its chelicerae and stabs it with its hollow pointed fangs, injecting a venomous fluid which brings instant death to the cricket and acts as a digestive juice. The tarantula macerates (reduces to a soft, easy-to-ingest state) its victim and then goes about "absorbing" its nutrients. If your tarantula does not consume the whole carcass, but only sucks it or partially eats it, don't worry. This is perfectly natural and happens quite frequently. Just make sure that when you clean your spider's tank you remove these dried-up remains. Your tarantula may take anywhere from twenty minutes (or less) to several hours (or more) to savor its prey. Often the tarantula will kill a victim but won't eat it; instead the tarantula quickly wraps the carcass in silk to preserve it, coming back to it later to enjoy the meal. After feeding, the tarantula usually walks away and cleans its fangs and chelicerae.

If your tarantula refuses food for some reason, as it might preceding a molt or when enduring the winter months, don't panic. All the tarantula needs is a little help. Take a small portion of dogfood or ground chuck and squeeze it into a tight, compact mass on the end of a length of string. Dangle it in front of your tarantula and shake the string to simulate the movement of live prey. The tarantula should attack and begin to devour the "victim." However, this method has met with only limited success. Many pet tarantulas, my own among them, are "wise" to this procedure.

Remember, your tarantula is best off when fed regularly. Although it can survive long periods without food, it is best to feed the tarantula every week and continue the feeding routine throughout the winter.

Because many pet tarantulas are desert-dwellers, they are somewhat accustomed to going without water for long periods of time. Indeed, you may never see your tarantula drinking from its water dish, as it gets the necessary moisture from its food. In over two years of tarantula keeping, I can recall seeing my tarantulas drinking from a water dish only six times. In experiments performed by Dr. William J. Baerg, one tarantula survived for seven months without water in a cool atmosphere, and another tarantula lasted 80 hot summer days. If you have a tropical tarantula, you should not let it go for more than a few days without water. Other species of tarantulas should receive fresh water at least once a week. In the summer months, rapid evaporation can prove to be a most annoying problem. Make sure that the water container is clean and that the water is changed often to prevent stagnation.

Your tarantula's water dish should be a shallow but sturdy container. I recommend that it be no deeper than half an inch. Probably the best dishes you can get are glass furniture casters. If these are not available, a shallow ashtray or jar lid should suffice. A cheaper though by no means permanent substitute can be made by cutting off the bottom of a paper cup. You can even use a moistened sponge or wet wad of cotton. Tarantulas will not experience any difficulty in obtaining moisture this way.

TARANTULARIUMS

One of the main concerns regarding tarantulas is their housing. The main problems in establishing a suitable home for your pet are safety and security, heating, and size. Since tarantulas are somewhat adept at devising means of escape from a tank, one must take special precautions. If you use fish tanks as your tarantulariums—and you should, because fish tanks offer many advantages—the tank cover should be weighted down or firmly attached. This prevents the tarantula from working its way out. Believe me, once tarantulas escape, they do their best to stay free. Some tarantula owners have had the good fortune to recover their lost pets after weeks or months or in some cases, more than a year. Remember, the time you spend in escape-proofing your tarantularium could save you worry over a lost pet as well as the price of a new one. As for heating, either keep the tanks in a sufficiently warm area of your house (which is what I have done) or buy a heating or lighting device separately and install it yourself. There is a device currently being sold in many pet stores which is a self-contained heating unit. It resembles a medium-sized brick and radiates warmth without the aid of an electric outlet. This item has been used successfully by some tarantula keepers and is worth checking into. For an approximate price and further information, check with your local pet shop.

Whereas some people derive great enjoyment from constructing homes for their pet tarantulas, many of us cannot work wonders with plywood, glass and some tools. I myself am certainly not mechanically inclined, and neither are many other tarantula enthusiasts. I realize that there is a certain joyous sense of accomplishment in designing and creating something useful. However, I prefer to buy my tanks ready-made.

In all my experience, I have seen tarantulas kept in everything from margarine tubs to cardboard boxes. I presently keep my tarantulas in various abodes; for the most part, I use clear plastic tanks (which come in different sizes) which feature removable ventilated covers. I also keep a 25-gallon high tank, a large Tupperware container and a clear glass fish bowl with a homemade wire mesh top. Perfectly spherical fish bowls are often used without covers; as the tarantula climbs upward in search of freedom (as it is certain to do) the pull of its own body weight forces it to inevitably drop before reaching the open space at the top. You can even make a simple but effective temporary tarantularium out of an empty jar with airholes poked in the lid. Ventilation usually isn't a problem; just make the airholes relatively small and widespread.

Overall, I feel the best container to get is a fish tank with a secure wire-mesh cover. In their eagerness to properly house their tarantula, pet owners often needlessly splurge on the size of the tank. Although a larger tank certainly makes a better display case, tarantulas do not require much living space. A five-gallon tank provides more than enough room. If you are as avid a collector as I am, you will probably amass tarantulas quicker than you can arrange living quarters. There is a relatively easy solution to this problem. Place a tank divider in one (or more) of your larger tanks. This enables you to keep more than one tarantula in each large tarantularium. As previously mentioned, tarantulas are cannibalistic!

Each spider must be kept in a separate enclosure for its own safety. Tank dividers come in various sizes to fit different aquariums and have proved quite effective. In short, fish tanks allow a great deal of creative license on the owner's part. They are secure, spacious, and convenient for display. Remember, the type of tarantularium you construct or purchase depends on how much time and energy, not to mention money, you are willing to put into it.

When preparing your tarantula's abode, it is important to consider which type of spider will be occupying it. A burrowing species such as the Mexican red-leg will probably construct a simple burrow. Most burrowing species are rather awkward climbers, so it might be wise to keep cage decorations and objects to a minimum, for the tarantula's protection. Other than a water bowl and perhaps a rock or two, I keep my tarantulas' tanks devoid of objects. My Mexican red-legs are somewhat unorthodox; they are excellent climbers and do not show much inclination towards burrow-building. If you keep a tree-dwelling tarantula, it would be a good idea to have some tree branches in its tank. Many pet shops stock dead branches, complete with base. Make sure that there are no sharp splinters which could pose a threat to the tarantula. I do not recommend going out and cutting your own branch; you run a risk of bringing parasites and other unwanted animals into your pet's home. Also, tropical tarantulas require higher humidity and temperature; about 75-80 degrees should be sufficient. North American tarantulas are usually better off at about 70 degrees.

There are a variety of substances with which to cover the floor of your tarantula's dwelling. I recommend the use of sterilized potting soil over the use of ordinary soil. This is just another precaution against parasites. I also suggest the use of a certain odorless, parasite-free gravel which is suitable for use by a tarantula. Many kinds of gravel, although intended for fish, can be put to good use for tarantulas. If you want your tarantula to dig a burrow (if it is a burrowing species) but it shows no inclination to do so, make the burrow yourself. You can create a fairly good burrow by pressing soil around a cardboard tube; this is passable and might even encourage the tarantula to improve upon it. I have heard of a graduate student in Arizona who catches tarantulas in the wild, makes a mold of the burrow, reconstructs the burrow in an enclosed backyard area, and returns the tarantula to its "new home." Tropical tree-dwelling species will probably construct their own nests, which are camouflaged silk aerial tunnels that connect with a hollow tree section or some other form of shelter.

The tarantula's cage should be cleaned whenever it needs to be, which is not often. I usually clean my cage once every three or four months. This cleaning, which begins after I transport the tarantula to a holding tank, consists of removing cricket remains, scrubbing the water dish, washing the inside and outside walls, and cleaning the cover. Since the tarantula excretes a quick-drying fluid, there is virtually no smell or mess.

HANDLING

Like most other pet keepers, the tarantula keeper usually purchases his pet with some intention of handling it. For some it is a learning experience; for others it is a means of conquering a fear that lurks within the dark recesses of many human minds. Upon buying a tarantula, one should not feel obligated to pet or fondle it. Actually, your tarantula is probably much better off not being held. As was previously stated, a tarantula requires little care, and being handled is not one of its physical needs. Consequently, you cannot under-handle your tarantula.

However, it is possible to over-handle a tarantula. Pets which have been frequently handled over a period of time have been known to strike with little provocation. I acquired one of my tarantulas for a rock-bottom price of $5.00 because it had developed a reputation for viciousness. I later found that its viciousness had, in fact, been caused by frequent handling.

There are a number of safe ways to handle a tarantula. There are also many methods of handling which could prove unsafe to both human and spider. One should always act with caution when handling a tarantula; many species are extremely quick. Although most American varieties, for instance the Mexican red-legs, are usually docile, tropical species tend to be rather nervous and jittery when held. No matter which type of tarantula you have, apply the same basic rules of caution.

Perhaps the safest method of handling your tarantula is to grip it securely between the second and third pairs of legs with your thumb and forefinger. The legs will probably thrash in the air, seeking something to latch onto as you lift the spider out of its tank. If the tarantula does touch something while being taken out of its abode, it will increase its efforts to escape. If you pick up the spider quickly and all eight legs leave the ground at the same time, the tarantula's reaction is to simply stop moving. A situation such as that of being lifted up never occurs in the tarantula's natural habitat, so this creature's nervous system is completely unprepared. Because the spider does not know how to deal with the situation, a self-induced paralysis sets in. Another method of picking up your pet is to nudge it gently into the palm of your hand or a temporary container such as a cup. All you need to push the tarantula is a stick, pen, pencil or finger. You just guide the spider along the desired path into whatever manner of container you decide to use.

Once the tarantula is in the palm of your hand, lift the hand slowly, taking care that the spider stays in one place. It is always a good idea to keep one hand positioned underneath the hand holding the tarantula. This is to give the tarantula something to crawl onto, rather than letting it wander aimlessly off your hand. If your tarantula is a persistent crawler, you may find yourself frequently changing hands to prevent the spider from falling. If the tarantula does stay put and doesn't take advantage of the opportunity to crawl up your arm, you should be able to carry it virtually anywhere within reason. But don't let your tarantula crawl all over you. . . having the spider crawl about on your person can prove fatal for the tarantula if it falls and painful for you if it bites.

Unfortunately, when it comes to tarantulas being injured or killed by falls, I speak from sad experience. My Mexican brown, Heinrich, died as a result of a fall during a demonstration in April, 1979. He was accidentally dropped from a height of about five feet, and his abdomen burst. Heinrich died several hours later, mainly due to loss of blood. Within a few days of this tragic incident, my Honduran tarantula, Attila, jumped from a partially open cage that I was carrying. From a height of about four feet, Attila leaped onto a patch of grass and scurried halfway across a parking lot before I recaptured her. Luckily, the only injury she sustained was a bleeding front leg joint. Successful treatments of coagulant and plenty of care proved the deciding factor in this case. One can well imagine the state of mind I was in that week; of my three tarantulas I possessed at the time, one had died and another had been badly hurt. The cases I have just mentioned clearly illustrate the fact that a tarantula controls its own destiny when it jumps from a relatively safe height; drop a tarantula from the same height and you run the risk of the tarantula's certain death.

If you are hesitant about handling your tarantula, don't worry. You should have plenty of time to become accustomed to this fascinating new pet. If you are unsure of yourself or concerned for your tarantula's safety, don't yield to the persistent requests of "Let it crawl on you" made by curious people who don't know any better. These all-too-frequent requests are to be expected by the owner of any unusual pet. Your pet's safety should remain foremost in your mind at all times. When you have come to the point where you feel comfortable with your tarantula, that is when you should handle it freely. Remember, safety-consciousness is to be admired; foolhardiness is to be avoided.

There is some danger involved in handling your tarantula. One of the most common questions I am asked is, "How can you handle it like that? Won't it kill you?" To begin with, I am always cautious when handling tarantulas, and this probably accounts for the fact that I've never been bitten. Tarantulas pose little threat to human beings and in fact are an invaluable aid in destroying harmful, crop-eating insects. The names I have chosen for my pet arachnids reflect the public's preposterous attitude toward tarantulas as menacing creatures. There's Genghis, named for the Mongol conqueror Genghis Khan; Attila, named after the pillaging chieftain Attila the Hun; Tamerlane, named after the Oriental conqueror whose empire was composed of half the known world; Himmler and his late counterpart, Heinrich, were both named after Heinrich Himmler, Reichsfuhrer and head of the dreaded S.S. of Nazi Germany; Mengele, named after Josef Mengele, the S.S. camp doctor at Auschwitz and now the most wanted Nazi war criminal in the world; Idi Amin, named after the infamous Ugandan dictator; and Vlad, my Arizona bark scorpion, named after Vlad Tepes, a real-life Wallachian prince whose grisly deeds inspired the book *Dracula*. As long as I keep pet tarantulas, I will continue to name them after infamous historical people. I could just as easily name them "Harry," "Spot," or "Fido," but this is my satirical way of showing how ridiculous and undeserved the tarantula's reputation is.

It is a fact that tarantulas are quite capable of defending themselves. The first measure of defense is withdrawal or retreat. If this does not succeed in discouraging the attacker, the tarantula then "kicks hairs." In other words, the tarantula uses its back pair of legs to repeatedly rub the abdomen and shake loose hairs, which it flings in the direction of the attacker. Certain types of tarantulas, including Mexican red-legs and Haitian blacks, fling clouds of hairs at anything that disturbs them. The bird-eating *Avicularia* tarantulas have poisonous hairs, which they weave into the layers of silk that make up their nests. This is certainly enough to discourage most predators, and it causes a painful yet temporary rash on humans. When flung, these poisonous hairs can cause blindness in a number of tropical predators, and they have been known to temporarily blind humans.

However, hairs do not have to be flung or used as nest barriers to cause harm. On two occasions, I have had a temporary rash on my neck and arms after handling my Genghis. Genghis had not kicked hairs on either occasion, and the rash disappeared in less than an hour. Several tarantula owners I know have experienced allergic reactions which necessitated the use of gloves when handling their tarantulas. After handling a bird-eating tarantula, a curator of the entomology section of the London Zoo experienced a severe allergic reaction. According to the *International Wildlife Encyclopedia*, this unfortunate handler's hand "was red, swollen and painful for several days and one of his fingers remained permanently crooked."

Now we come to the root of the tarantula mystique—its bite. From time to time throughout history, various studies have been conducted as to the effect of the tarantula's bite. Jean Henri Casimir Fabre (1823-1915), the renowned French naturalist and author of the 10-volume classic *Souvenirs Entomologiques,* carried out a unique experiment using European tarantulas. Undaunted by tarantula folktales, Fabre's test showed that while tarantula venom brought about nearly instant death in insects, a small sparrow dies within roughly 72 hours, and a mole took approximately a day and a half to die. Fabre's conclusion was that a tarantula bite could prove harmful to humans and that steps to produce an antidote to the venom should be taken. Keep in mind, however, that these studies used European "tarantulas"—hardly more than glorified wolf spiders. Recent tests show that true tarantulas, especially tropical species, can kill reptiles and large rodents in less than an hour.

In northern Australia, two species of dangerously venomous tarantulas roam about in some of the more remote areas. *Atrax robustus* and *Atrax formidablis* range from 30-40 millimeters in length; they have rather large fangs and are extremely nasty. They are small specialized tarantulas which construct funnel webs in which they trap hapless insects. Fortunately, comparatively few people come in contact with these fairly poisonous spiders.

Most people mistakenly believe that the venom of a tarantula is deadly to humans. Recently I had the privilege of speaking to Dr. Gertsch of Portal, Arizona. He is 73 years old, has been handling spiders for 50 of those years, and has come in contact with numerous tarantulas during that time. He revealed that in all those years of study he has been bitten about 20 times by tarantulas. Most of these bites were, as he put it, caused by "careless handling." None of the bites was serious, although at first there was some "sharp pain and a little blood." Dr. Gertsch's work has been done primarily in the southwestern United States and Mexico.

The bite of nearly all tarantulas is about as harmful as a bee sting. True, the tarantula is venomous, but its venom was designed to bring down prey smaller than itself. In fact, with the exception of one family, *all* spiders are venomous. Unlike the brown recluse (now found throughout the U.S.) and the infamous black widow (also well dispersed), tarantulas have never been known to kill a human being with their venom.

However, there are a few people who have experienced allergic reactions to the bite of a tarantula. The most severe cases I have ever heard of required hospitalization. In most of these rare cases, there was some vomiting and feverishness. Allergic reactions to bee stings kill people every year, so don't take chances on a tarantula bite. If you're bitten, treat the wound as you would a normal puncture. Clean the wound and use antiseptic to prevent infection. The injury may throb and ache for some time, and there is the possibility of nausea and a fever. Whether you are allergic (which you might not know until you're actually bitten) or not, seek a *professional* opinion as soon as possible.

Like a rattlesnake, the tarantula also gives a warning sign before attacking. It rears back on its two pairs of back legs and exposes its fangs. If this defiant gesture does not discourage the intruder, the tarantula will then strike. This consists of snapping the vertical-moving jaws, driving the sharply pointed fangs into flesh by means of a stabbing motion, and injecting the venom through the fangs into the tissue.

In short, the tarantula bite normally poses little threat to human beings. However, since the possibility of allergic reaction remains, use caution when handling your tarantula. If you feel hesitant about handling your tarantula, then don't; chances are you might wind up harming the tarantula. Remember, a tarantula can be a very rewarding pet *if* you use proper judgment when handling it.

It is very important that you look closely at your tarantula so you can recognize a broken leg (left) or a possible infestation by parasites (see below). Photos by Dr. Herbert R. Axelrod.

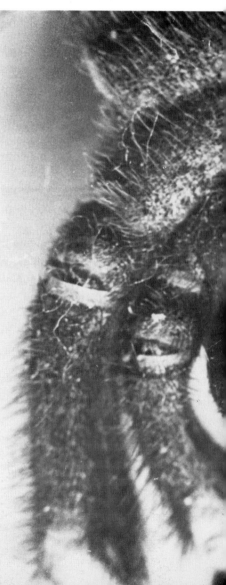

Keeping Your Tarantula Healthy

One of the important things to know about your pet tarantula is how to treat the various illnesses and afflictions that are bound to spring up at the most inconvenient times. Most of the ailments are not serious, but it pays to be prepared. The times when a tarantula requires the most observation are: during the molting process; whenever, if ever, you decide to breed your tarantulas; and on those hopefully rare occasions when misfortune strikes your spider in the form of an accident.

It is somewhat difficult to determine exactly when something's amiss in the world of your tarantula. A tarantula sits still for long periods of time; when it does move voluntarily, it usually crawls at a rather slow pace. Often a tarantula will "play possum" at the most inopportune times. During one pet show, Attila refused to move at all at judging time. Don't be worried if this happens; the tarantula is simply saving energy. Believe me, when a tarantula wants to move quickly, this stored energy comes in handy. Once, when I was filling the water dish in Attila's tank, she shot up my arm in the manner of an Olympic sprinter. This taught me never to underestimate the speed of a tarantula—its sluggish demeanor can be deceiving!

Temperature plays a vital role in maintaining the well-being of your tarantula. Make sure that the tarantula's tank is between 70-80 degrees Fahrenheit. This is ideal for the hardy, easily adaptable Mexican red-legged tarantulas. If you own a tropical tarantula, make sure that the tank is closer to 80 degrees. Spraying some water around the tropical or tree-dwelling tarantula's webbing helps maintain a humid, jungle-like atmosphere. Recreating the tarantula's natural habitat plays an important part in keeping your spider healthy.

During the winter months, I usually keep my tarantulas close to the radiator. Some species, the Mexican red-legs for example, possess unique metabolisms that provide for slow growth as well as the ability to slow other body functions during winter. While not as extended as the hibernation period of higher animals, this semi-dormancy enables the tarantula to survive without food or water for relatively long periods of time. During the winter, keep fresh water in the cage at all times and offer food every once in a while. As previously stated, tarantulas will eat at their own rate.

During the summer months, certain precautions must also be taken. If you decide to devote some time to suntanning and want your tarantula to keep you company, watch it! Although the majority of tarantulas kept as pets are desert-dwellers, they have their limits, too. Remember that tarantulas are nocturnal; the hot day is usually spent in a burrow, and the cool night is used for hunting. Keep your tarantulas out of direct sunlight—it can kill them! On one occasion Attila, whose tank was mistakenly placed in the rays of a hot August sun, suddenly keeled over on her back and drew her legs inward. Fortunately, I noticed this in time and rushed her into the shade. Within a half hour, Attila was successfully revived. Another problem which poses a very real danger to tarantulas is a radical change in temperature.

If you look in your tarantula's cage one day and notice that it looks dried-up and has a somewhat shriveled abdomen, it is probably dehydrated. Give the spider fresh water as soon as possible. I have had only two instances of dehydration among my tarantulas; both occurred after the tarantulas were delivered by mail. A little fresh water easily solves this problem.

Many ailments happen as a result of molting. Prior to molting, your tarantula might refuse food. Several weeks before molting, small droplets of a clear fluid have been noticed seeping from various leg joints on the spider. Don't be worried whether you observe this or not; it does not happen to all tarantulas, as far as I know. Molting is a difficult, strenuous experience for your tarantula. According to Rick West, who is currently engaged in writing his own tarantula book, "Molting increases the blood pressure in a tarantula by almost twice its normal pressure. The increase in blood pressure is dependent on how much body fluid it had inside it at the time. If the body fluid or blood pressure is low, either due to dehydration or bleeding, then the limbs will be unable to move and the abdomen will be misshapen."

Your tarantula will probably be tender, soft, and extremely sensitive after molting, so it is wise not to handle it until about a week after it molts. Be sure to keep fresh water and food nearby, for the tarantula usually has a voracious appetite after molting. This is to replenish the energy expended during the molting process. One of the very real dangers of molting is the possibility that your tarantula might bleed to death. Since tarantulas have virtually no coagulants or clotting factors in their blood, death resulting from loss of blood sometimes happens in the wild. If you notice your tarantula bleeding from a leg joint, dab the wound lightly with a coagulant-covered cotton swab. Vaseline has been known to work in some cases, but check with a medical authority first. On the other hand, if your tarantula is bleeding from a gash on the abdomen or the carapace, you are practically helpless. In these instances, because of the possible damage to vital organs, wounds do not mend easily. It is best to treat the cut like any other wound; let the tarantula's natural recuperative powers take over, and hope for the best. However, in cases of severe wounds (such as those sustained in a fall) there is usually little chance of recovery. Due to the slow metabolism of the tarantula, death usually takes place after a prolonged period.

Another very real danger confronting your tarantula is the existence of parasites. There have been cases in which a fly of the family Phoridae, which resembles the common fruit fly in size, could possibly have caused the death of several tarantulas. I discussed this briefly with Alice Gray of the Department of Entomology, American Museum of Natural History. She has had several tarantulas, not to mention other arachnids, die as a result of infection caused by these awful parasites. Some tarantula keepers have noticed small, worm-like appendages protruding from the abdomens of their pets. The only possible deterrent I can recommend is that you check for parasites every so often and keep the cage as clean as possible.

Following cases of both successful and unsuccessful matings, there is the possibility of conflict between male and female tarantulas. As mentioned before, NEVER put two or more tarantulas in the same tarantularium (unless you're breeding them, of course). Except for the South American red-toe tree-dwelling tarantula, I know of no other tarantulas which can live together in harmony. Injuries sustained in combat with other tarantulas are often fatal. Their slow metabolism enables them to linger for awhile, and some tarantula authorities feel that the most merciful thing to do is put the spiders out of their misery.

If you notice your tarantula working its chelicerae up and down, or if you see it rubbing its cephalothorax with its hind legs, don't worry. Your pet is just cleaning itself. If you notice that your tarantula's abdomen is getting darker than usual, don't panic. Darkening of the abdomen is one of the signs of molting. If you observe a bald spot developing on your pet's abdomen, there is no need to worry. Due to a frequent flinging of hairs, it is perfectly natural for your tarantula to develop a bald spot.

There is no cause to worry if your tarantula is missing a leg. Lost appendages are regenerated, or grown back, during the molting process. These new limbs are often smaller than the originals. They are often less wieldy than the originals as well.

Among the other miscellaneous injuries that could affect your tarantula is a blockage of the digestive tract. This can cause death.

In short, injuries and afflictions can be prevented or cured if you take proper action. I must emphasize here that there is pitifully little knowledge concerning tarantula illnesses. Since you know your tarantula best, a combination of past experience and common sense will hopefully rectify the situation. If that proves inadequate, I am sure that the advice, preventative measures and treatments described here will be of great aid in keeping your tarantula healthy.

Your tarantularium can be made attractive, as well as interesting, by decorating it with cactus and other plants. Photo by Dr. Herbert R. Axelrod.

An old aquarium, such as that shown to the right, is ideal for setting up as a tarantularium. It isn't easy to breed spiders of any type, but it's possible if you start with a healthy, attractive male and female spider, such as the female shown above hovering watchfully over its eggs.

Breeding Your Tarantula

Perhaps the most challenging aspect of keeping tarantulas is to attempt to breed them. This is an extremely difficult and demanding task, even for the most learned tarantula enthusiast. It has been accomplished by Dr. William J. Baerg, Mr. Arthur Bordes and Mr. Richard Blauman. I myself have wanted to breed my tarantulas for quite some time now but have been unsuccessful in all attempts.

Earlier in this book, I recommended that tarantula enthusiasts purchase an immature male or female, for purposes of longevity. However, if you find yourself with an adult tarantula, I would suggest purchasing a mature spider of the opposite sex. After all, there are certain advantages to breeding tarantulas. After a successful mating, you could have hundreds of tiny spiderlings. With the market for pet tarantulas booming as it is, you could earn a tidy sum of money by selling the baby tarantulas. In addition, the sense of achievement to be gained by rearing tarantulas knows no limits. A tarantula owner can learn fascinating new things by helping to bring about a successful mating.

The first step in breeding your tarantulas is to acquire healthy adult specimens. When looking for a male, check under the joints of the front legs for mating "hooks." The presence of these hooks, which play an important role in the mating process, is the sign of a mature male tarantula. Also check to see that the spinnerets and pedipalps are undamaged. If the male has numerous bald patches, missing appendages, or a faded, "knocked around" appearance, he is probably too old to mate. As for the opposite sex, it is often difficult to tell the difference between females and immature males. However, in many species the female has a fatter, more developed abdomen.

Once you have two healthy specimens, you must wait until the time is right. Most mating seasons last from September to October, but some tropical species begin as early as spring. Keep close watch on all molts prior to this period, because after this molting an immature male tarantula will acquire mating hooks. After this "molting milestone," the male will need several weeks to recuperate, produce sperm and prepare himself for mating. When the female is ready, she gives off a relatively far-reaching scent which can be detected by roving males. The male then constructs a sheet of silk, upon which he deposits some sperm. He will then dip his pedipalpi into the sperm.

As soon as the male fills his palpal bulbs (those bulbous configurations on the ends of the pedipalpi) with sperm, he is ready to go. I would advise that you feed your female prior to mating; if she is full, she will usually be too sluggish and slow to attack the male. Attempting to breed tarantulas is a real gamble, because the spiders may attack each other both before and after mating. It would be best to keep a stick or barrier (sheet of cardboard) handy at all times for purposes of prying them apart. Once these preparations have been made, you can put the male into the female's tank; it must be the male who visits the female's tank and not the other way around. This is the way it occurs in nature, and it is vital to the success of the mating. It is also important that there be no noises that would distract the tarantulas.

In most species, it is the male who directs the proceedings; Mexican red-legs are good examples of this. However, in many tree-dwelling tarantulas the female is more active. The male will send the female into a trance-like state with a constant vibration of his legs. He will then secure her fangs with his mating hooks, raise her front legs and bare her genital slits. Once this is accomplished, the male will usually insert first one palp and then the other. After he has discharged his sperm, he will withdraw the palp and, carefully but swiftly, get away from the female, who has by this time "awakened"—usually in a nasty mood. Separating the tarantulas at this point will prevent a fight. When you separate the spiders, DO NOT USE BARE HANDS. Both tarantulas are still quite agitated, so keep a stick available to prod the male into some kind of temporary container.

The fallacy persists in the mind of the public, and even among many tarantula enthusiasts, that a female tarantula will always kill the male after mating. This so-called fact is based on scattered observations of isolated matings. In the wild and in captivity, the male often survives to mate more than once. Although violence can erupt, either prior to mating, during the action or immediately afterwards, it usually doesn't. Conclusions may have been drawn from watching an old, impotent male tarantula attempt to mate with a larger and stronger female. Naturally, the male is killed or fatally injured for his efforts, but an occurrence such as this shouldn't stimulate people to conclude that this is the usual outcome. Certainly fatalities often occur in the wild, but they are by no means the rule. The case of the black widow spider, which derives its name from the female's "habit" of killing her mate, is similar. I doubt that tests involving hundreds of matings have been undertaken in order to correct the public's mistaken beliefs. In the wild as well as in captivity, the male tarantula will most likely live to mate several times.

After his first mating, the male tarantula will live anywhere from a few months to slightly over a year. Again, this post-mating lifespan depends on the species. Mexican red-legs, which take quite some time to mature, rarely live for more than seven or eight months after reaching adulthood. Continue feeding the male well; perhaps he will construct another sperm web and be ready to mate again, with the same or a different female.

The female tarantula, on the other hand, is burdened with the task of rearing offspring. She should also be fed well so that the production of eggs goes smoothly. If all has gone well, in less than a week the female will make a patch of silk on which to lay her eggs. Depending on the species, a female can lay anywhere from 60 or 70 eggs to 600 or 700 eggs. In many tarantulas, such as the Mexican red-legs, more than 400 eggs are laid. Once the female has laid all her eggs, she will form the patch of silk into a loose, bag-like container for the eggs. Many tarantula authorities feel that certain foods are necessary for the female to produce a fine, healthy egg sac. These "cravings" range from June beetles to small crickets to moths. Personally, I feel that a female tarantula should have a varied diet at this time. This will hopefully ensure that certain nutrients will aid in the construction of an egg sac.

The female tarantula will jealously guard this egg sac until the baby spiders, or spiderlings, hatch. This usually takes about two months, but don't be alarmed if it takes longer. When the spiderlings do hatch, they resemble tiny whitish replicas of the adult tarantulas. Mexican red-leg spiderlings are rather dark and do not acquire their stunning coloration until they are about 18 months old.

The spiderlings should be separated soon after hatching to prevent fatalities inflicted by the mother as well as by fellow "sac-mates." I would recommend feeding the baby tarantulas small, slow-moving insects. A tiny section of sponge soaked in water should be kept in each tarantula's cage. Housing itself is a serious problem, because hundreds of containers are required. With the proper care, the tarantulas should reach maturity in three to ten years, depending on the species. Some tropical tarantulas may take less than two years, and certain Mexican species require more than eleven years. Some conditions in captivity, such as temperature, have been known to slow down a tarantula's growth. Females generally mature later than males and live several years longer after reaching adulthood.

NOTE: Breeding takes a great deal of patience. If you are not able to take the time necessary for such an endeavor, I would advise abandoning your plans. Breeding also requires quite a bit of financial sacrifice, as each spiderling must be fed and housed separately. Don't take on the challenge and responsibility of rearing tarantulas unless you consider yourself qualified and prepared in all respects.

The female tarantula zealously guards her egg sac, so don't try to grab her.

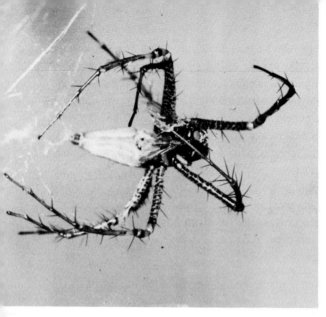

There are hundreds of different species of spiders (such as the one shown above) that are suitable for the home hobbyist, but there also are some (such as the black widow spider at right) that are dangerous. If you trap some harmless local spiders, you can use them as the basis of breeding experiments.

Tarantulas And Human Culture

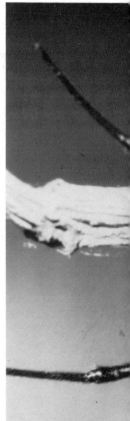

It is only fitting that a creature as graceful and widely distributed as the tarantula should become firmly established in many diverse cultures throughout the world. Like many other animals, tarantulas have become integral parts of tribal folklore and in some places are even revered as deities.

From the Caribbean Islands come the many tales of Anansi, who is Jamaica's answer to "Br'er Rabbit." Anansi is depicted as half-man, half-spider, and able to change back and forth at will. Anansi is a cunning, wily fellow whose mythical exploits have been told to innumerable West Indian children over the years.

The giant *Lampropelma* tarantula from Malaysia is considered a god in its home country. It has an 8-inch legspan and is more commonly addressed (by reverent Malaysians) as "Earth Tiger."Ironically enough, in the same part of the world tarantulas are also much in demand—not as gods, but as food! The in-

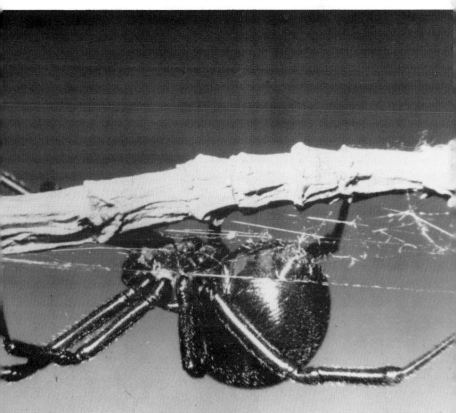

habitants of Thailand, Annam, Cambodia and Burma, as well as certain places in South America, greatly relish the taste of fresh tarantula.

The tarantula has not been ignored in literature, either. I am not referring to lurid dime-novels that glorify the "killer" image, but to early "scientific" studies. In *Comity of Spiders*, W.S. Bristowe gives one of the earliest and most detailed accounts of the tarantula's mating ritual. In the book *Anatomy of Melancholy*, published in 1621, Robert Burton advised hanging a tarantula or large wolf spider in a nutshell around the neck. This was supposedly a cure for malaria, dating back to ancient times. The wonders of medical science! Personally, I feel even chicken soup has more basis in fact.

But by far the greatest effect of tarantulas on human culture was the "tarantism" craze of the Dark Ages. This outbreak, similar in fervor to the 'dancing madness' which swept Europe years later, spawned the popular Italian folk dance the tarantella. The outbreak of mass hysteria had its roots in Taranto, Italy, and started in the early 15th century. According to the legend (which encouraged the belief that tarantulas seek out human "victims"), after being bitten by the tarantula, the victim had to whirl about in a frenzied dance. This exhausted the person, but at the same time ' cured ' him. It was not uncommon for a single villager to ' spread ' the affliction to the rest of his community. Indeed, whole provinces were affected by such a chain reaction. The so-called tarantula responsible for these outbreaks was a species of large European wolf spider, *Tarantula narbonensis*.

The "less civilized" North American Indians dealt with the problem of tarantula bite in a much more effective, if less sensational, manner. Natural plant remedies were used to alleviate the pain of tarantula bites. The Navajo Indians concocted a tea of the fendler bladderpod to combat tarantula wounds. The Hopi Indians used wild sunflower on these spider bites. The Blackfoot Indians treated tarantula bites with a moist poultice of crushed western wood lily flowers. In Texas, prickly pear cactus dressings have been used for years to combat the effect of tarantula and scorpion bites. Many of the secrets and exact applications of these native remedies have been lost for ages, so I would advise seeking modern treatment.

TARANTULAS AND THE MEDIA

Although tarantulas pose little or no threat to human beings, various media such as television and movies constantly portray them in a radically different light. The public's incessant exposure to the opinion of those who don't know any better makes it a relatively one-sided battle. The number of movies, such as *Tarantula, Kiss of the Tarantula* and the more recent *Kingdom of the Spiders,* as well as TV movies like *Tarantulas: The Deadly Cargo,* greatly outweigh the number of documentaries and television programs such as *Wild World of Animals.*

The movie *Kiss of the Tarantula* was one of the worst offenders of the "killer-tarantula" genre. In it, a girl shuns the company of peers, wicked stepmother, lecherous uncle and kindly mortician father in favor of keeping a basement full of tarantulas. The image of a person who keeps pet tarantulas really takes a beating here! The girl, something of a female "Willard" substituting tarantulas for rats, kills her stepmother and some classmates, as well as her uncle, all with the aid of "deadly tarantulas." This is certainly a horror movie—a horror for any tarantula owners to watch! Other movies of higher quality, such as the James Bond tale *Dr. No* and the more recent *Dr. Scorpion,* utilize judgement worthy of low-budget "B" movies. In *Dr. No,* James Bond escapes death at the fangs of another "deadly" tarantula. In *Dr. Scorpion,* an evil scientist peddling military secrets relaxes by pitting scorpions against centipedes and by watching tarantulas scare the daylights out of unfriendly agents.

Television comedies have also been quick to capitalize on the tarantula's fearsome reputation. In an episode of *The Brady Bunch,* Peter (played by Christopher Knight) is petrified at the sight of a tarantula crawling up his bedsheets to his chest. Peter's brother Greg brushes the tarantula to the floor, where it is coaxed into a paper bag and disposed of. All this happens while the family is vacationing in Hawaii. In an episode of *Get Smart,* "superspy" Maxwell Smart gets rid of a menacing tarantula by killing it with a jar of horseradish. Only in the syndicated series *Please Stand By* is a tarantula depicted as a pet. The pet spider escapes, causing some humorous situations.

The Brazilian huntsman spider (shown above) and the African baboon spider (below, eating moth caterpillars) are, like the scorpion shown on the facing page, potentially dangerous arachnids. All three are venomous.

The newspapers and magazines have lately been giving more and more coverage to the members of the American Tarantula Society. These members have spoken out in local as well as national newspapers and have received coverage in magazines ranging from *Playboy* to *People*. Dale Lund, founder of the American Tarantula Society, for instance, has also appeared on local television and radio shows. Some national magazines have also published articles concerning the rise in popularity of exotic pets. Tarantulas have been mentioned favorably in these articles and have even been featured on at least one cover!

Comic Billy Crystal, of *Soap* fame, has included in his comedy routine a spoof of the old jungle movies in which tarantulas were depicted as villains. This act was recently featured on the *People's Command Performance*. Altovise Davis, who co-starred with William Shatner (of *Star Trek* renown) in *Kingdom of the Spiders*, made an appearance on the Johnny Carson show. Mrs. Davis, who was accompanied by her famous husband, entertainer Sammy Davis, Jr., also brought along a pet tarantula to illustrate the harmlessness of these spiders. Needless to say, Mr. Carson was somewhat flustered at having a tarantula roam freely upon his desk and person.

While vacationing in Arizona, former world heavyweight champion Rocky Marciano and his wife Barbara encountered a tarantula in the bedroom of their cottage. She screamed at him to come quickly and dispose of the "bug." Rocky immediately dashed into the room. Upon seeing the tarantula crawling along the floor, the fearless (and undefeated) veteran of 49 fights, with 43 victories by knockout, jumped on top of a dresser. Finally giving in to his wife's frantic pleas to kill it, Rocky threw one of the dresser drawers at the unfortunate spider, crushing it instantly. This incident was witnessed by Ernest Clivio, a Massachusetts businessman and longtime friend of Marciano's, and is also described in Everett M. Skehan's biography of the late champion.

So far, stardom has eluded my own tarantulas. Two free-lance photographers expressed a great deal of interest in using my Mexican red-legs for an advertising campaign, and an agency that contracts animals for commercials, movies and television is considering signing on my tarantulas. Most of the proposals are still in negotiation (nothing definite as of this writing), but who knows? Maybe someday one of my spiders will receive a "Patsy" (the animal version of the "Oscar")!

TARANTULAS: AN UNRECKONED INTELLIGENCE?

We have all, from time to time, heard documented accounts of remarkably intelligent pets—dogs, cats and even horses. Unfortunately, tarantulas have never been considered geniuses. However, recent experience prompts me to speak out in their favor. I have noticed that Genghis, one of my two Mexican red-legs, welcomes the visit of my hand into his cage. At first I thought this was a simple Pavlovian reflex or an anticipation of food. I tried having someone else put their hand in the tank; Genghis crawled away. I do not consider myself enough of an authority to venture a scientific opinion. My only guess is that the hairy little guy likes me!

I have heard of other tarantula owners whose pets have been similarly trained. One tarantula was trained to respond to the blast of a whistle. For those of you who enjoy delving into the paranormal, I know of at least one case in which telepathy was experimented with. As the tarantula owner held her tarantula in the palm of her hand, she made a mental decision to put the spider back in its tank. Nearly every time this was done, the tarantula moved closer to its owner, perhaps sensing the action she was about to take and not wanting to return to its tank. Whether you believe it or not, it is certainly intriguing.

One of the most remarkable cases it has been my privilege to learn of is the instance regarding a certain Mexican red-leg. This "super-spider" has been known to sort out small heaps of gravel. The only unusual thing is that each pile is a different color! Multi-colored gravel was poured into this tarantula's tank, and 24 hours later the Mexican red-leg began putting gravel of one color in one pile, gravel of a different color in another heap, and so on.

How much of this behavior is instinct and how much is intelligence? How does a tarantula gauge the speed it will take to overtake and kill a cricket? The answers to these and many other questions lie no farther than your tarantula's tank.

On the right is a beautiful thorn spider from South America. It is a highly visible animal and is easily spotted. The yellow spider shown above, however, is well camouflaged and almost looks like a part of a flower. It awaits insects attracted to the blossom and seizes them for food.

THE AMERICAN TARANTULA SOCIETY

The American Tarantula Society was founded by Dale Lund, the author of *All About Tarantulas*, in late 1977-early 1978. In its first two months, the society attracted 42 members in the United States and Canada. From this modest beginning, it grew to its present size—495 members in 36 states, 4 Canadian provinces and Holland. I am now its Director.

It began as just a passing dream, a thought gnawing at Dale Lund's mind. After his popular and authoritative book was published, incoming letters of inquiry from readers convinced Lund that there were more spider people out there than he had reckoned with. These people were asking for an organization, something to belong to. So the American Tarantula Society was born, thanks to Lund, his family and a small but dedicated group of tarantula enthusiasts.

The people that make up the American Tarantula Society come from all walks of life—doctors, clerks, students and housewives. They vary in age from a seven-year-old, who is saving up to buy his very own pet tarantula, to a 93-year-old doctor who has been involved with tarantulas since 1918. I myself am proud to be a member of the Society. No matter how limited his experience with tarantulas, each member is welcome to contribute to the club's bimonthly newsletter, the *Tarantula Times*. This newsletter contains the personal experiences of tarantula owners; notes on different tarantula species; updates concerning the club's progress; profiles of outstanding members; questions and answers from members; cartoons, poems, puzzles and artwork that readers contribute; advertisements; and news concerning the projects and activities of the club members. Dale Lund serves as editor, but the newsletter comes alive through the contributions of the Society members.

In order to become a member of the American Tarantula Society, one need not actually possess a tarantula (although nearly all members have at least one). An interest in tarantulas is all that is required. Members are given a membership card and badge, both decorated with the club logo: a tarantula perched on top of the globe. Upon becoming a member, one receives the club newsletter and has the opportunity to purchase back issues. Members may place ads in the newsletter and have the chance to contact other members through the convenience of a membership directory. Details about membership, including information about current costs of membership, can be obtained directly from the ATS; requests for information should be accompanied by an addressed stamped envelope. Write to:

American Tarantula Society
564 Boulevard
New Milford, N.J.
07646

Besides the Lund family, outstanding members include Dr. William J. Baerg, author of the book *The Tarantula* (now out of print) and one of the most esteemed tarantula authorities in the society; Alice Gray, of the American Museum of Natural History, a well-known entomologist; and Ann Moreton, founder of the National Arachnid Society and owner/operator of the Spider Museum, as well as many others.

All members can help realize the goal of the American Tarantula Society, which is to bring about a better understanding of this misunderstood creature, the tarantula, as well as to erase the stigma of years of bad publicity.

THE WORLD'S LARGEST SPIDERS-THE BIRD-EATING TARANTULAS

According to the *Guinness Book of World Records*, the largest spider ever captured was a male South American bird-eating spider *(Theraphosa blondi blondi)*. Its body was 3½" long and weighed nearly two ounces, and it had a legspan of 10 inches. It was found at Montagne la Gabrielle, French Guiana, in April of 1925. In the same article, the heaviest spider on record is mentioned. This was a female long-haired tarantula *(Lasiodora klugi)* captured at Manaos, Brazil, in 1945. It weighed nearly 3 ounces and had a 9½-inch legspan.

Found mostly in South America, bird-eating tarantulas are not common in the United States as pets. I myself am the proud

The *Guinness Book of World Records* says that the largest spider is a South American bird-eating spider, shown above. The African baboon spider, on the facing page, might be a runner-up.

owner of Mengele, a South American "red-toe." The bird-eating tarantulas are not as easily handled as North American tarantulas. They are quick and extremely nervous when held, and they are bound to run up an arm or off a hand. To protect the tarantula, keep handling to a minimum. In captivity, these arboreal (tree-dwelling) tarantulas require tree branches for climbing and building silk shelters in. A humid atmosphere with water constantly available should be provided. Bird-eating spiders will eat whatever your other tarantulas eat—crickets, grasshoppers, small mice, etc. They tend to be shorter-lived than most tarantulas; some species rarely live beyond four or five years. Many bird-eating tarantulas differ from their North American cousins in terms of size. Whereas many American species are rather bulkily built, the bird-eaters tend to be more slender, with longer legs. While most American tarantulas seldom exceed five or six inches in legspan, the bird-eating spiders average about seven inches across the legs.

Bird-eating tarantulas can often be found prowling the Amazon jungle at night in search of insects, small mammals and baby birds (hence the name). Upon emerging at dusk from their silk-lined aerial retreats, bird-eating spiders hunt down their meals. When the prey is caught, the tarantula stabs it and injects its venom. Before the unfortunate victim completes its death throes, digestive juices begin to liquefy its body. It may not be a seven-course dinner, but it satisfies the tarantula. When the spider comes across an animal it can't handle, it usually resorts to flinging its poisonous irritant hairs. These hairs have repulsed attackers many times the size of the tarantula. Bird-eating spiders have also been known to place poisoned hairs between the layers of the nests in which they keep their young.

Bird-eating tarantulas go about mating with the same difficulties that other types of tarantulas face. After a period of time, which varies according to species (but usually is several months), the female lays her eggs. Again, the number of eggs varies according to the species; as few as 20 or as many as 1000 eggs are laid at a time. These eggs are placed in a silk shelter and are guarded jealously by the female. It should be mentioned here that the seasons in which these events take place also differ from species to species. The eggs hatch after a varying period of time, and the newly emerged hatchlings usually enjoy a short time of parental care. The hatchlings eat small insects at first but quickly move on to larger prey. The lifespan of bird-eating tarantulas changes with every species you study. They have been known to live less than five years and up to seventeen years. However, according to the *International Wildlife Encyclopedia,* statistics show that not more than 0.2% of all bird-eating spiders reach maturity.

The feeding habits of bird-eating tarantulas were first described in 1705 in the book *Metamorphosis Insectorum Surinamensium,* by Maria Merian. In one chapter was an account telling how these tarantulas hunted and killed young birds. Unfortunately, the book was scorned and ridiculed by the unbelieving zoological community. It wasn't until 1863, more than a century and a half later, when eyewitness reports corroborated her story, that Merian was given the credit due her.

If you want to keep more than one spider in an aquarium, the aquarium can be partitioned with a tank divider. Your pet store can help you with everything you need. Trust your pet dealer; if he doesn't keep your pets alive and healthy, he won't have a business.

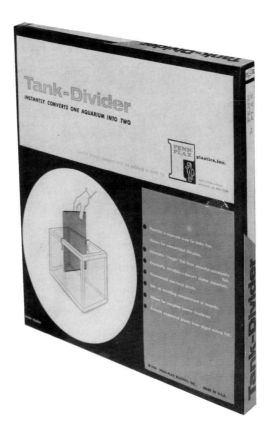

Exhibiting
Tarantulas

It all started on a typically uneventful Friday afternoon. As I was reading the evening newspaper and playing with my favorite tarantula, Genghis, I came across a full-page feature on the annual Bergen County (New Jersey) 4-H Fair. Skimming through the decidedly boring article quickly, several phrases in particular suddenly reached out and grasped my attention: "Open pet show"; "Ribbons awarded to top entries"; "All varieties of pets eligible". A wide grin spread across my face as I looked from the words "All varieties" to my pet tarantula, Genghis. Why not, I figured?

Up to this date there hasn't been an International Tarantula Exhibition, but lots of communities have pet shows. If you own a beautiful tarantula like the one shown on the facing page then you might be able to win some awards like those shown with the author (below)—but not until it had regenerated its missing leg.

I spent the rest of Friday and most of Saturday eagerly preparing. I cleaned the tanks of Genghis, a young male Mexican red-leg, and Attila, a female Honduras black velvet, and Heinrich, a male Mexican brown. I scrubbed their water dishes, removed the remains of numerous crickets and made bright nametags for each spider's tank. I also typed up information cards containing interesting facts about tarantulas and designed a poster showing the various life-functions of tarantulas. As a final touch, I washed my tarantula T-shirt.

The morning of Sunday, July 16, 1978, dawned bright and clear on Overpeck County Park in Leonia, N.J. I stepped out of the car and hefted the large cardboard box containing the three tanks as well as the poster. My 75¢ entry fee (25¢ per entry) safely tucked away in my pocket, I made my way to the registration booth. The official in charge, a balding, middle-aged gentleman with the bored look of someone carrying out a routine duty, gave me a registration form. I paid the entry fee, filled out the form, and handed the sheet back to him.

"Tarantulas!" he exclaimed. My back stiffened and my jaw set as I prepared to defend the virtues of keeping pet tarantulas.

"Well, looks like this is going to be an interesting contest, after all. S'pose you'll be a shoo-in for most unusual." I nodded, thinking back to the form I had just filled out. There were six categories: dog, cat, rabbit, guinea pig, mouse and "other." Contestants in this category of "other" were eligible for the awards of "Most Unusual," "Prettiest," and "Most Tame." Of these three, "Most Unusual" was by far the most prestigious.

I gathered up my arachnid companions and walked across the fairgrounds, attracting strange looks from the numerous passers-by. Upon entering the tent, I immediately set up my tarantulariums and the colorful poster. A crowd composed of 4-H officials, other entrants and people enjoying the outdoor fair soon formed.

For the two hours left before judging, I talked, handled my tarantulas and answered questions. The most common ones were "Why don't they bite you?" "Are they really as dangerous as they are in the movies?" "How can you touch them—do they know you?"—and the inevitable "Why do you do this?" I also listened to such responses as "Wow," "Yecch " and the extremely rare "Beautiful!!"

My initial apprehension melted as judging time rolled around. I was still attracting sizable groups of people and was feeling reasonably sure of myself. My confidence faded somewhat as I saw a late entrant setting up his display. I gazed in dismay at what he had brought, three large boa constrictors! The crowd's attention, which I had dominated up until this point, instantly shifted to this newcomer as the judging finally got under way.

I showed off Genghis, Attila and Heinrich to the best of my ability. Unfortunately, the three judges were obviously not well acquainted with spiders, having subtracted points for Heinrich's "missing" leg ("You mean he's not supposed to have nine legs?") My rival with the snakes, Tony Penn, knew that he and I were the only contenders for the coveted award. As we tensely awaited the results, I exchanged nervous glances with my rival who had exhibited the boa constrictors.

"It'll be close," I said.

"Yeah, right down to the wire," he replied.

Finally the results were announced. In the midst of booing and scattered cheers, Tony Penn and his boa constrictors were declared the winners of first place in "Most Unusual." My tarantulas came in second place. Inwardly, I seethed at the poor judging, but I congratulated Tony and collected my green second place ribbons, which were dwarfed by the large blue ribbon and rosette awarded to Tony.

Driven by that defeat, I vowed that I would return in triumph next year. I became a member of the American Tarantula Society and founded my own business, Tarantula Enterprises. After the untimely death of Heinrich, who was accidentally dropped by a biology teacher, I acquired two more tarantulas. I was determined to be ready this time.

Sunday, July 15, 1979, finally arrived. Once more I journeyed with my tarantulas—Genghis, Attila, Idi Amin and Himmler—to Overpeck Park. With a calm look of experience evident on my face, I registered. I paid the entry fee, which had doubled (that's inflation for you!). I then went to that familiar main display tent to show my spiders. Just like last time, a crowd gathered. I notic-

Crab spiders, like the one shown above, on the facing page and on page 70, are so well camouflaged that they are not readily seen by their prey or their enemies (including people). The one above has just captured a butterfly.

ed a few familiar faces among spectators and contestants alike, including the confident countenance of Tony Penn. My old nemesis had indeed come prepared. He brought an eight-foot Burmese python named Caesar, which he exhibited well. I didn't do badly myself. I generated a good deal of interest in my growing business as I handed out my business cards to prospective clients and curious judges. The demonstration proceeded flawlessly, and the exhibition was more polished and a great deal more sophisticated than the previous year's.

Needless to say, Tony Penn and I were nervous about the judges' decision. The judges arrived at last, pausing only to award the blue ribbon for "Prettiest" to a parakeet. Tony and I stood side by side, anxiously awaiting the verdict. My heart sank as a blue ribbon was handed to Tony. As I turned to congratulate him, a blue ribbon was attached to Genghis' cage and my outstretched hand was pumped vigorously. The judges, upon noticing my mixed happiness and astonishment, explained that while Tony Penn and his python had won "Most Tame," Genghis and I had won the most important title, "Most Unusual." TRIUMPH AT LAST!!

TIPS FOR ENTERING YOUR PET TARANTULA IN COMPETITION

KNOW WHICH CONTESTS TO ENTER: There are not many open pet contests, sad to say. Most pet shows are exclusively for dogs or cats. Your best bet is to keep your eyes peeled for the annual or semi-annual pet shows put on by your local organizations (V.F.W., Jaycees, Elks, etc.). Another good idea is to watch for the sadly infrequent 4-H or County Fairs, which usually include an open pet show among their many other attractions. Yet another thought is to be aware of the rare pet events put on by schools, libraries, pet shops and churches. In any case, make sure that the contest is for *all* pets. If the coordinators of the competition advertise it as such, they are legally bound to accept your entry, no matter how unique, as long as it is displayed safely and with no risk of injury to other contestants or spectators.

KNOW HOW MUCH TO PAY: Pet shows which admit all kinds of pets are rarely, if ever, staged for profit. The pet shows that my tarantulas have entered were put on or sponsored by non-profit organizations. Most other fund-raisers and similar events charge some nominal entry fee, usually just to cover costs of prizes and so forth. At any rate, when you're competing for a relatively cheap ribbon or badge (I realize that the honor has no price tag), it doesn't make much sense to pay more than a dollar (at most) per entry. Believe me, when you're entering groups of tarantulas, it can add up!

BE RESPECTFUL TO AND TOLERANT OF JUDGES AND SPECTATORS: Even though judges are often ignorant in matters pertaining to tarantulas, their decision is final, so be courteous. While you're busy presenting an intelligent, comprehensive and hopefully interesting demonstration, you might even educate the judges. As for spectators, their support can be encouraging and even influential to the judges. In order to win their backing, courtesy and patience, as well as an entertaining exhibition, are very important.

KEEP SAFETY IN MIND THROUGHOUT YOUR DEMONSTRATION: The safety of your pet, not to mention that of the judges and spectators, should be foremost in mind. Don't let visions of glory cloud your better judgement. To impress the crowd, one need not give in to requests to handle one's pet in a hazardous fashion.

KNOW WHAT CATEGORY TO ENTER: It would probably prove a waste of time to enter your tarantula in a category such as "Best in Show" or "Prettiest." Go for something that you stand a good chance of winning, such as "Most Unusual."

PRESENT THE CORRECT VIEWPOINT AND THE PROPER FACTS: Since tarantulas are relatively harmless, why spread the myths about the spider's bite? Don't encourage ignorance; if you keep pet tarantulas, make your viewpoint known. As a person who knows better, it is up to you to help destroy the

If you enter tarantulas in competition, you can be sure the judges will probably refuse to handle them. Don't try to force people to hold a tarantula, as they might panic and drop the poor spider, killing it upon impact. The spider on the facing page is a poor specimen. It is balding and aged. Photos by Ron Reagan.

Kathy has two large tarantulas which she has put into one old aquarium (which leaks, by the way and is not good for fishes). She would never think of leaving them alone together.

Kathy handles her tarantulas very, very carefully. She knows that they can deliver a painful bite and that they are generally better off if not handled at all. Photos by Dr. Herbert R. Axelrod.

The spider illustrated above is among the most dangerous of spiders and is called the black widow spider. Black widows have a wide distribution and are common in the southern United States. Tarantulas (on the facing page) are best not handled. They may not be able to kill you, but why take chances of having a severe allergenic reaction? Besides, tarantulas can be made mean-tempered by excessive handling.

Different people react in different ways to tarantulas. The lady on the opposite page, for example, seemed curious enough to give them a close examination, while the lady above simply smiled—and walked away. Photos by Dr. Herbert R. Axelrod.

false image and overblown notoriety that have plagued tarantulas to this day.

In conclusion, I would just like to emphasize that tarantulas make wonderful pets. Keeping tarantulas has been and (hopefully) will continue to be an enriching, vastly rewarding experience. The writing of this book has enabled me to reach a higher level of maturity and dedication.

As I wrote this book, the impact finally hit me; many other people get as much enjoyment out of keeping tarantulas as I do! I would like to end this book on a note of gratitude; thank you, tarantula enthusiasts everywhere, for the courage and dedication to maintain your unique interest.